Gleanings

FROM THE

Garden

Lessons learned in the garden
about life and the Lord

By Jason L. Belcher

Word of His Mouth Publishers
Mooresboro, NC

All Scripture quotations are taken from the **King James Version** of the Bible.

ISBN: 978-1-941039-51-9
Printed in the United States of America
©2024 Jason L. Belcher

Word of His Mouth Publishers
Mooresboro, NC
www.wordofhismouth.com

Table of Content

Introduction

As I have spent a number of days and hours working in the garden over the years, I have learned a lot. While I cannot say that I am a professional gardener by any stretch, I certainly enjoy trying to raise and manage a garden. I enjoy the challenge of taking a little seed and putting it in the ground and caring for it, then watching it grow up into something that bears fruit that you can take from the garden and put on your table to eat. I have learned a lot in the garden just by the mistakes that I have made and by hands-on experience. Of course, nature itself and the ground have taught me many things as well, just learning the way of the garden the old fashioned way. Certainly, there are plenty of books pertaining to gardening out there, but as is the case a lot of times, we learn the most the hard way. Among all the gardening lessons I have learned, I have always taken notice of the comparison and the connection that many of these same garden lessons apply to us in spiritual ways as well. Therefore, comes this little book in which I hope to highlight some of the lessons that I have learned and gleaned from working in the garden. God absolutely uses nature to teach us things about Him and about life in general, and I hope you find these lessons from the garden to be a blessing and an encouragement to you.

Chapter 1
The Garden of God

God is a gardener; it plainly says so in Genesis 2:8. *"And the Lord God planted a garden eastward in Eden and there he put the man whom he had formed."* Once God had made the first man, Adam, this is where God put him, in the garden. This is the first garden that there ever was, the garden of Eden. But the Bible has a lot more to say about gardens. The word "garden" appears in the Bible over 50 times. Evidently, God thinks a lot of the garden. The Bible uses the "sowing and reaping" garden analogy numerous times, as well as many references to the soil, the seed, and the harvest. Certainly, there is much for us to gain from things pertaining to the garden and all of its illustrations.

From the very beginning, God intended the garden to be used for food and for man to eat from.

Genesis 2:9, *"And out of the ground made the LORD God to grow every tree that is pleasant to the sight, and good for food…"* Some of the healthiest, best food for our bodies that you can ever eat comes right out of the garden. God made it just for us because He knew what our body would need to get all the vitamins and nutrients we need. God knows how to take care of us even physically, and He has provided a wonderful and inexpensive way to feed our bodies and get what we need straight from our own garden.

You can remember sitting at the table with your mom or dad telling you how important it is to eat your vegetables so you can grow up big and strong. Well, it turns out that it is true. Those foods from the garden give us so many health benefits, and God knew what He was doing when He put them there for us. It is just another sign and indication of His love for us.

The garden is also an active, growing, flourishing place where life and fruitfulness can be found, Genesis 2:9 *"…the tree of life also in the midst of the garden…"* We know that all life and all living things can only come from the giver of life. Be it the life of a plant, tree, human, or any other creature. All life comes from Him. John 15:5 reminds us, *"I am the vine, ye are the branches: He that abideth in me, and I in him, the same bringeth forth much fruit: for without me ye can do nothing."* John 1:4, *"In him was life…"* When we see the garden breaking through the ground and springing forth with new life, it is simply a reminder of the gift and the blessing of life that can only come from the Creator.

God planted a garden, He placed a man in His garden, and He provided for that garden as well.

Genesis 2:10, *"And a river went out of Eden to water the garden…"* Before God creates something, He knows everything that it will need so it can be taken care of. He understands this garden will need water so therefore He puts a river by it to supply its needs. That is another beautiful picture of how God knows our needs before we do and that He has taken care of everything that we will ever need if we will just look to Him. God is a thorough God who has all wisdom. Matthew 6:32, *"… for your heavenly Father knoweth that ye have need of all these things."* Whatever your need is, He knows, and He will supply our needs. All we need to do is to seek Him and He will help us, for He delights in helping His children.

God also gave Adam the task and responsibility to protect that garden and to care for it. Geneses 2:15, *"And the LORD God took the man, and put him into the garden of Eden to dress it and to keep it."* God intended for him to work and gave him a job to do in the garden. If you have

9

a garden, you understand how much work is involved. Of course, this garden that God put Adam in at the time was a perfect garden. There were no weeds, no thorns, and the ground had not yet been cursed by the fall of sin. Still, though, there was work to do. God creates us, but He also gives us a job to do.

Notice also how God's presence could also be found in His garden as well. Genesis 3:8, *"And they heard the voice of the LORD God walking in the garden in the cool of the day: and Adam and his wife hid themselves from the presence of the Lord God amongst the trees of the garden."* Genesis 3:10, *"And he said, I heard thy voice in the garden…"*

God enjoys His creation, and He enjoyed His perfect garden that He had made. We see how God took a stroll through His garden to look upon it and to enjoy it and see all the wonderful things that He had made. God is in His creation, and He is found in nature everywhere you look. God is in the outdoors.

There's just something about going outside, going out in nature, going in your garden, and somehow feeling closer to the Lord. I used to go on top of a high mountain with some church friends, and we would look out over miles around and into the dark starry night and we would begin to pray. It just felt different and like we were more in tune with God. God speaks to us through His creation and it stirs our soul and resonates deep within us. Like Adam said, *"I heard thy voice in the garden."*

I, too, can say that God has spoken to me a number of times when I was outside working in the yard or in the garden. God has shown me many things through His natural creation, and if you will just be sensitive to the Spirit of God, He will speak to you as well. God is there far more than we realize or take the time to recognize. He desires to speak to us and to have that sweet fellowship with us more than we can ever understand. God made us for companionship.

Soon, though, the serpent would enter the garden, and Adam and Eve would disobey God by eating of the forbidden tree and fall into sin. This was the day that God cursed the ground, and we have been suffering the consequences of sin ever since. Genesis 3:17 *"...cursed is the ground for thy sake; in sorrow shalt thou eat of it all the days of thy life; Thorns also and thistles shall it bring forth to thee; and thou shalt eat the herb of the field; In the sweat of thy face shalt thou eat bread, til thou return unto the ground..."*

God was now forced to banish Adam and Eve from the perfect garden that He had made, and the perfect ground would be now cursed and filled with thorns and thistles. We are going to see a little later on how much of a problem this is going to become for the ground of our garden.

Though man messed up God's perfect garden, God had a plan to fix it all, and it would be in His Son Jesus Christ. Jesus would come and be the innocent and spotless sacrifice for our sins. Before Jesus would go to the cross to pay the ultimate price for sin, I don't think it is a coincidence that Jesus, just before He was betrayed by Judas found Himself in a garden, the garden of Gethsemane. (John 18:1) Nor is it a coincidence that near where Jesus would be crucified there was, yes, a garden. John 19:41 *"Now in the place where he was crucified there was a garden; and in the garden a new sepulchre, wherein was never man yet laid."* Yet, we cannot forget that when Jesus gloriously and victoriously rose over death, Hell, and the grave, it was near a garden. As Mary came that morning to anoint His body with spices, she saw the angels and, wondering at what was going on, turned around and thought it was, *"the gardener"* (John 20:15) until she realized that is was Jesus who had called her by name. It was in a garden where Adam fell into sin and the curse of death was cast upon all men. However, it was also in a garden where Jesus defeated sin and paid the price for us to be given life.

Oh, how much the Lord has in store for us to learn from the garden experiences in Scripture. Oh, how much we can glean from the Word of God through the illustration God has given us in something so simple as a garden. Yes, God is a gardener; in fact, He is the chief and master gardener, and He has much to teach us not only about a physical garden in our yard, but more so, in the garden of our heart and life.

Chapter 2
The Soil and the Soul

Once you have decided to have a garden, and after you have picked out a good, sunny and preferably flat location, one of the very first things you have to do is to begin working the soil. The soil is critical, and it must be prepared for your new garden. In order to have a successful garden it is essential that you have good soil to work with. This will require the help of some useful hand garden tools, a good tiller, or even a tractor, depending on the size of the garden that you are going to have. Tools and equipment will be necessary in order to do any gardening.

As gardening needs the necessary tools, in order to be successful in our life and to bear fruit, we also need some tools. One of the main tools that we will need also fits in our hands, and it is called the Bible. God has given us His Word as the guide for life. It is our blueprint, our instruction map. It will teach us all about God, the master gardener, and how He wants to work in our lives if we will let Him. Of course, in order to get the most benefit out of it, we must open it up and refer to it regularly. Many times, we think we don't need the instruction manual and when we try to live life without the instruction manual of the Word, we end up in a mess. So don't forget to read the manual; it is quite an important tool for success.

God has also given us the tool of prayer. This tool is quite effective and profitable in our lives, and if we are to have a fruitful Christian life, we will need to employ this most valuable tool as well. Without using the proper tools, we just simply won't be able to accomplish much in our life with God. Just as a builder must have tools to do the job, the gardener must also have the essential tools to have success.

Now begins the work of preparing the soil. Every gardener knows that in order to plant a garden, you first need to make ready the soil where you will soon plant your seeds and plants. You cannot just go out in the backyard and toss seeds around and expect everything to work out for you. You need soft, fertile soil that has been plowed up, chopped up and turned over and made ready for planting. Any ground that hasn't been used in a while becomes hard, and if you are dealing with a piece of land that has never been tilled before, it will be full of all sorts of things that will hinder you in your gardening. I am thinking here of things like grass, weeds, roots, and stony rocks; all of these things must be removed before you begin to plant anything.

> *"Farmers know that so long as the land is hard and cloddy, the seed has no chance to get the nourishment by which it lives; besides turning it over, the plough exposes that which has been hidden to the light of day, and it is by turning it up that it gets the benefit of the atmosphere. The nitrogen contained in the air is filled with that which the growing seed requires to find in the land, if it is to do well for the worker. Have we not thirty-fold crops where we ought to have an hundredfold, for want of better ploughs? The heathen who spoke of preaching as "turning the world upside down" hit on the truth; and those of us who fail to turn up the soil are not likely to reap all we might."* Thomas Champness

Plowing the ground and turning up the soil is like preaching. When you go to church, the preacher begins to unapologetically open up the

Word of God and plow the gospel plow and expose the sin that lies within us and call us out to turn from it, repent of it, forsake it, and get rid of it in our life. This is the importance and value of preaching. We must turn up the soil!

The prodigal son returned back home when he "came to himself." This refers to him repenting or turning from his own way and coming back home to the father to make things right again. The Bible tells us in Romans 2:4 *"...that the goodness of God leadeth thee to repentance."* Preaching is God's way of calling men and women out in their sin, helping them to realize their sinful condition, and drawing them (John 6:44) to Himself in love that He may forgive them and offer to them His mercy and grace. Preaching is a wonderful thing; it is essential, and a necessary thing that reveals our condition and points us to the remedy that is in Jesus and the cross of Calvary.

I Corinthians 1:18 *"For the preaching of the cross is to them that perish foolishness; but unto us which are saved it is the power of God."* Without the powerful preaching and plowing of God's Word, we will not have the harvest of souls or enjoy seeing the fruit of men, women, boys, and girls being saved by the transforming power of God from darkness to light.

As a tiller breaks up and turns the soil, so the preached Word of God turns us. Without plowing, we will find great difficulty in planting the seed, and without preaching, we will not have good soil to work with. Along with preaching, the prayers of the saints are also working to soften those hearts that may be hardened by sin. Many a saint has prayed and prayed for the heart of a loved one to be softened and to turn their life to the Lord. They witness, they invite them to church, they pray for their loved one to receive the gospel and wait for the day that they turn their life to Christ. Though prayer is oftentimes behind the scenes in the background, it is, in fact, working to soften the soil and work in the heart.

Matthew 6:4 teaches us that *"...thy Father which seeth in secret himself shall reward thee openly."* God sees and hears your prayers, so don't give up praying, because the more you pray, the more that soil in that hard heart is being worked into good, soft, fertile soil that can receive the seed of the gospel.

We must be diligent to do our part to help make the soil ready, it must be prepared to receive the seed that will soon be planted. As the saint is praying and as the preacher preaches, the seed of God's Word is ready to find good ground wherein to take root. Prayer and preaching help us to identify and remove the rocks and roots of sin that may have taken hold in our lives.

As I prepare and work the garden soil and get rid of these hindrances, I'm also reminded of what the Bible says about breaking up the fallow ground.

Jeremiah 4:3 *"For thus saith the Lord to the men of Judah and Jerusalem, Break up your fallow ground, and sow not among thorns."* Hosea 10:12 *"Sow to yourselves in righteousness, reap in mercy; break up your fallow ground: for it is time to seek the Lord, till he come and rain righteousness upon you."*

> *"The expression, 'Break up your fallow ground,' means, break off all your evil habits; clear your hearts of weeds, in order that they may be prepared for the seed of righteousness. Land was allowed to lie fallow that it might become more fruitful; but when in this condition, it soon became overgrown with thorns and weeds. The cultivator of the soil was careful to "break up" his fallow ground, i.e., to clear the field of weeds, before sowing seed in it. So says the prophet, "Break off your evil ways, repent of your*

sins, cease to do evil, and then the
good seed of the word will have
room to grow and bear fruit."
(Easton)

The people of Israel were sinful; they were stiff-necked and hard-hearted. They were a rebellious people who did not obey God but went their own way. They had become careless, idle, and had allowed the ground of their heart to become corrupted and filled with unrighteous things. God sends His messenger with the message that it is time for them to turn away from their iniquity and their wickedness and to turn back to the Lord. It is time to "break up" the fallow ground; it is time to turn back to the Lord.

Oh how prone we are to sin and to allow our own hearts to be polluted with the things of earth! It won't take very long before we are in danger of becoming calloused, hardhearted, unfruitful, and have a life that is filled with things that do not please the Lord. Therefore, we must make every effort to keep our hearts soft and tender before God and be quick to repent when sin comes into our lives. When the Lord convicts us of sin, we should not hold on to it but should confess it and make it right with the Lord, and do all that we can to keep our hearts pure and clean. As the psalmist said in Psalm 51:10, *"Create in me a clean heart, O God; and renew a right spirit within me."* We should ask the Lord to help prevent us from having a stony heart but a heart of flesh that is moldable and workable and can be conformed into the desire He has for us. Keeping the soil of our heart as well as the soil of our garden clear of sticks, stones, weeds and roots will be vital to what comes out of it later down the line. Clear your soil of the junk and debris that you find in it, and clear your heart of the things that seek to contaminate and fill it with sin. Plow and break up the ground and seek to eliminate the things that do not belong in it. By doing these things you will have good soil that can be worked in.

One more thing I would like to call your attention to regarding the soil before we move on. You might say, "Why are you spending so much time on the soil?" The soil is the most critical part, and it is foundational. If you are going to build a home, we understand that the most important part of that home will be its foundation. The soil is our foundation, therefore it requires great attention in order for your garden to thrive.

Jesus, in Mark 4, is teaching His disciples, and He tells them about the parable of the sower. Jesus often used parables to help those He taught to understand the message He was trying to get across. Jesus used an illustration that they could relate to to help them see the point.

Mark 4:2-12 *"And he taught them many things by parables, and said unto them in his doctrine, Hearken; Behold, there went out a sower to sow: And it came to pass, as he sowed, some fell by the way side, and the fowls of the air came and devoured it up. And some fell on stony ground, where it had not much earth; and immediately it sprang up, because it had no depth of earth: But when the sun was up, it was scorched; and because it had no root, it withered away. And some fell among thorns, and the thorns grew up, and choked it, and it yielded no fruit. And other fell on good ground, and did yield fruit that sprang up and increased; and brought forth, some thirty, and some sixty, and some an hundred. And he said unto them, He that hath ears to hear, let him hear. And when he was alone, they that were about him with the twelve asked of him the parable. And he said unto them, Unto you it is given to know the mystery of the kingdom of God: but unto them that are without, all these things are done in parables: That seeing they may see, and not perceive; and hearing they may hear, and not understand; lest at any time they should be converted, and their sins should be forgiven them."*

Jesus here listed four types of ground that the seed fell upon. Why is this important? Because as we have already mentioned, the ground or the soil is the most critical component to the seed.

The first place the seed fell was by the wayside. Occasionally, as you begin to plant seeds in the ground, some may fall out of your hand or out of the bag that you didn't mean to. They may fall to the ground and be difficult to find. Though we may not find and recover them, it surely won't take long for a bird nearby to spot the exposed seed and devour it. These seeds will certainly not even begin to take root or develop in any way. This ground is unplowed and hard ground. It represents a hard heart that will not receive the gospel. There is nothing wrong with the seed, but it is the soil that is at issue here. This reminds us again of the importance of soft soil and praying for soft hearts to receive the seed.

The next kind of ground Jesus mentions is stony ground. As we have already mentioned, stony soil will not make for good soil. Though there may be some soil on the top of the ground, just below the surface is stone. It would allow enough soil to plant a seed but not enough for roots to grow and develop to make it continue growing, and it will be easily consumed by adverse weather conditions.

This soil can represent those who heard the word of God and received the message of the gospel. They may have walked the aisle to an altar or made a profession or commitment to follow Christ, but it didn't last. As soon as their friends or family heard of their newfound decision, or as soon as difficulty or trouble came, they could not be found anymore. They flamed out after a short time because they had no root. They may have made a profession without a possession. A true indication of following Christ is whether or not you continue in the faith.

The third type of soil is considered thorny ground. This kind of ground may be suitable for seeds to grow in, but other things such as thorns, thistles, and other damaging things are growing there as well. It is ground that becomes crowded and chokes out the good seed. This type of ground can represent the other competing interests of earth that seek to rob us of bearing fruit unto the Lord. These thorns can be things like riches, pleasures, and cares of the world, things that take our time away that could be given to the Lord. This soil becomes unfruitful. The enemy will do all he can to distract us with everything else to see to it that we remain ineffective. As long as we are not producing fruit, the enemy is pleased and has accomplished the goal of choking out the good fruit. Fruitless Christians are useless Christians.

Finally, the last type of ground we see is called good soil. This kind of ground is soft, and it is clear of anything that would hinder or destroy the seed. It is plowed, fertile, and is in the best condition for the success of the seed. We can see this type of soil representing the individual who has placed their faith and trust in Christ. They have genuinely placed their faith and trust in Christ, and He has begun a good work (Philippians 1:6) in their heart that lasts. It is a faithful and fruitful individual that is growing in the grace and in the knowledge of the Lord Jesus Christ. (II Peter 3:18)

Jesus has given us a marvelous description here of these various types of soil that may exist in the heart of man. In order for the heart of man to receive the seed, his heart must first be good soil, tender and ready to receive it.

Good soil is imperative. Any farmer or gardener knows that in order to have a successful harvest, you cannot have hard ground, stony ground, or thorny ground. You must break up the fallow ground, get rid of the hindrances, and start with good ground. Without proper and prepared soil, your garden will not turn out the way you hope for it to.

Chapter 3
The Sower and the Seed

Now that your garden area has been plowed, tilled, and cleared of hindrances, comes the fun part. This is where you begin to decide and design what will be in your area. It is like a blank canvas, and you can now plant whatever it is that you would like to and then watch it grow. This space that now lies as simple dirt will soon be springing forth with life, and as you plant the seed, you can just see the potential that lies in this field.

When I begin to plant my own garden, I get out a piece of paper and draw out the rows and what and where I would like to plant everything. It helps me make a plan of how much room I have to work with and where exactly I planted things in the early going. Of course, you can also use garden markers as well to identify where everything is when the plants are just beginning to sprout up. This map is my blueprint for the garden. If I'm unsure where something is, all I have to do is refer to my garden map.

The Bible is our map; it is our guide. When we need direction and guidance, all we need to do is refer to it to help us know the way. God has a plan and a purpose for us as well. Our life is like a clear canvas from the time that we are born, and when God looks at us, He sees an exciting opportunity for spiritual life, growth, development, and fruit. What is now spiritually void of life has the potential to soon be bursting forth with life, new life in Christ.

As the rows are ready, this is where we begin dropping the seed or sowing the seed into the ground at the proper depth and spacing. You can sow as much or as little as your heart desires. I generally plant a wide variety of things, but I always plant more corn than anything else since I love to eat fresh corn straight out of the garden. There is nothing better than a fresh ear of corn on your dinner plate, knowing it came right from your own garden.

Since I want to have a large harvest of corn, I realize that I need to plant a lot of corn seed in the ground. Now, you may plant something else in more quantity than I do, but I plant more corn than anything else. I will also plant other things in smaller quantities based on what my family and I generally like to eat. However, I always plant with the idea already in mind of giving out and sharing with others more than I will eat on my own. I enjoy being able to share the harvest with neighbors, friends, and others. Therefore, I must plant bountifully the seed that I want the most return from, and obviously plant lesser of things I want smaller amounts of.

It is just the same as what the Bible teaches us in II Corinthians 9:6, *"But this I say, He which soweth sparingly shall reap also sparingly; and he which soweth bountifully shall also reap bountifully."*

You will get out of your garden what you put into it. If you plant a lot, you will have a much better opportunity for a bigger harvest. If you only plant a few seeds, you will only get a little back in return.

It is much the same in our life. We get out of it what we put into it. I can't expect to reap what I never sow. If you plant nothing, then you will surely reap nothing. Neither can I expect to plant green beans and reap a watermelon. You reap what you sow. If you want beans, plant beans; It is quite simple.

So many times we may look at our life and wonder why things are not developing. We must ask ourselves the hard questions and examine what we are sowing. It may be that we are sowing sparingly yet expecting to receive an abundance. If we put in the time, work, and effort and do everything within our power to see fruit growing in our life, then we have a much greater chance of seeing that take place. Too many times, we may settle and become lazy and half-hearted, but if we truly want to see results, we have to be willing to pay the price and give it our whole heart. We reap what we sow.

The Bible is very clear about this in Galatians 6:7-9, *"Be not deceived; God is not mocked: for whatsoever a man soweth, that shall he also reap. For he that soweth to his flesh shall of the flesh reap corruption; but he that soweth to the Spirit shall of the Spirit reap life everlasting. And let us not be weary in well doing: for in due season we shall reap, if we faint not."*

The Bible gives us two very different and contrasting results of the seed that is sown. Whichever one you feed the most will win. Whichever one you sow will be the result you get every time.

> *"This figure is taken from agriculture. A man who sows wheat, shall reap wheat; he who sows barley, shall reap barley; he who sows cockle, shall reap cockle. Every kind of grain will produce grain like itself. So it is in regard to*

30

our works. He who is liberal, shall be dealt with liberally; he who is righteous, shall be rewarded; he who is a sinner, shall reap according to his deeds." Albert Barnes

When we sow to the flesh and to our sinful appetites, that is what we will reap. The apostle Paul, under the inspiration of the Holy Spirit, gives us these examples of the works of the flesh that we need to stay away from: Galatians 5:19-21 *"Adultery, fornication, uncleanness, lasciviousness. Idolatry, witchcraft, hatred, emulations, wrath, strife, seditions, heresies, envyings, murders, drunkenness, revellings, and such like..."*

If a man is unable to control his anger and kills someone, he will reap the consequences before the judge. If a man eats unhealthy day after day, sooner or later he will develop health problems. He can't blame God or anyone but himself for his result. If a man drinks and drives, he can't be upset with the police for arresting him; he sowed that seed, and he got what it produced. If a man is lazy and calls out of work too many times, he has no reason to be angry with the employer for firing him. He brought it upon himself.

These are what I call self-inflicted troubles. No one wakes up in the morning wishing to receive trouble, but if our ways and our actions are only sowing seed that produces undesirable results, stop sowing that seed. Sooner or later, the chickens come home to roost. If we don't like the fruit of the seed, plant better seed. The fruit is not the problem; it's the seed that was sown. Therefore, plant good seed.

Though we may tend to think of this verse in Scripture in a negative way, it has two sides to the coin. It is not only, "Hey buddy, you're going to reap what you sow if you keep up those bad habits," it is likewise also true that if we sow to our self good seed, we will reap good fruit. If a student studies hard, they are more likely to get a good grade. If you are faithful and give your best at work, you may receive recognition, a pay raise or even a promotion. If a man obeys the traffic laws and doesn't speed, he will keep a clean and clear driving record, perhaps even a discount on his car insurance for safe driving. Good actions beget good fruit and good rewards.

When we sow to the Spirit, the things of the Spirit, we reap the same. When we live unto the Lord, follow His ways and obey His Word, God honors that. Walking in the Spirit produces positive results in our life.

Galatians 5:22 *"But the fruit of the Spirit, is love, joy, peace, longsuffering, gentleness, goodness, faith, meekness, temperance, against such there is no law."* If we are led by and walk in the Spirit of God, we will enjoy the fruits of what it produces. When we invest and spend time in the things of the Lord and in His Word, we are sowing seed to the Spirit. The Lord blesses that seed and time with Him, and we grow more and more in Him. As He teaches us, speaks to us, and we yield to Him He leads us into life everlasting.

Who is the sower? We are the sower. Like it or not, every one of us is sowing some kind of seed everyday of our life. It may be good seed or it may be bad seed, but we are sowing something all the time. What kind of seed are you sowing in your life? Is it seed that is sown to the flesh, that which reaps negative things, or are you sowing seed to the Spirit that produces good things? Whatever you sow is what you will reap.

Another picture of the sower here is anyone who casts the seed of God's Word. When we preach, we are casting forth the seed of the Word of God. When you share Christ with others, you are sowing the Word. As disciples and followers of Christ, we are all called and commanded to be sowers; it is not only the preacher's job. The preacher can't reach everybody by himself, but we can sow seeds to the people whom we are around. Together, we can be an army for the Lord, casting the seed of God's Word everywhere we go. Ask God to help give you boldness to share the good news with those you are in contact with.

The Scripture refers to the seed as the Word of God. Luke 8:11 *"...The seed is the Word of God."*

Once you have begun to plant and sow the seed of your choice in your garden, make certain that you cover up the seed in the loose soil. This prevents, as we touched on earlier, a nearby bird from coming and snatching the seed away. These birds are like Satan, who wants to devour the seed as soon as it is discovered. Satan hates that seed! Why does he hate it so much? Because he knows the power that it possesses. Though a seed is such a small little thing, it has great affect, and it has great power according to the Scripture. Hebrews 12:4, *"For the Word of God is quick and powerful, and sharper than any two-edged sword, piercing even to the dividing asunder of soul and spirit, and of the joints and marrow, and is a discerner of the thoughts and intents of the heart."*

The Devil does not want that seed taking root in the heart of man. He hates God, he hates His Word, and he wants to remove God and His Word in every way that he can. Why do you think there is such an attack on the Word of God, or why do those who are anti-God seek to remove the Bible from public schools and other public places? The enemy knows the power of the Word of God and that it can change and transform men's hearts and lives. It opens their eyes to sin and causes them to turn from it. It turns them from darkness into God's marvelous light. The more we read God's Word, the more we hear it, it pierces our hearts, and reveals our need for Christ. The more we dwell and meditate and marinate on the seed of God's Word, the more it grows on us and in us and it begins to bear fruit in our life, and the Devil does not want that to happen.

This seed of God's Word is unlike any other seed. This seed doesn't corrupt like other physical seeds will. This seed produces eternal life, according to I Peter 1:23, which says, *"Being born again, not of corruptible seed, but of incorruptible, by the Word of God, which liveth and abideth forever."* Over time, those garden seeds will decay; they can turn bad and lose their effectiveness. However, the seed of the Word of God will never lose its power. It will never decay; it has and will continue to stand the test of time as Matthew 24:35 declares, *"Heaven and earth shall pass away, but my words shall not pass away."*

Despite the best efforts of the enemy and those who seek to eliminate the seed or the Word of God, it will never happen. God has preserved His word, and it is forever settled in Heaven. (Psalm 119:89)

When that physical seed gets in the tender soil, it begins to take root and it begins to grow up into a much greater plant. It is just amazing what one little tiny seed can turn into. Look at how Jesus described the power of one little tiny seed to His disciples. Matthew 13:31-32 *"Another parable put he forth unto them, saying, The kingdom of heaven is like to a grain of mustard seed, which a man took, and sowed in his field: Which indeed is the least of all seeds: but when it is grown, it is the greatest among herbs, and becometh a tree, so that the birds of the air come and lodge in the branches thereof."*

Have you ever held a mustard seed in your hand? I have, and it is such a tiny seed that you think, "Surely this can't amount to anything." Yet this tiny thing has the power to grow into such a big thing. As I begin to plant my seeds in the garden, some of them are so fine as little bitty grains, but my, how they can produce such tremendous results and growth!

Never underestimate the power of one simple little seed. It is imperative that we cast the seed of God's Word into the hearts of men any and everywhere we go, for we just never know what that one seed could produce in the heart of one soul who is ready to receive it.

How do we cast the seed? There are many ways. One does not need any special skill or ability to spread seed. Don't be fearful and afraid to tell someone about the Lord. One of the best ways to spread the seed is just by telling others what Jesus has done for you. Perhaps it is by putting a gospel tract into someone's hand or in a prominent place in public somewhere. It may be by witnessing to a friend, family member, or co-worker. Sometimes, people will even "open the door" for an opportunity for you to talk to them about the Lord. If people see you living your life for the Lord, at some point, they will have a need in their life and they just may come to you and ask for your prayers. Then you can sow that seed of the gospel in kindness and compassion, and we just never know the difference that it may make in their life.

I have also learned that in order to expedite the process of the seed beginning to sprout, you can soak the seed before planting it in the ground. This soaking of the seed works to soften it and help the seed germinate faster.

As we go about sowing seeds of the gospel, when we sow that seed with tears it will help that seed to be softer as well. When we see our loved ones and those around us who need to be saved, it ought to burden us and move us to tears. Psalm 126:5-6 *"They that sow in tears shall reap in joy. He that goeth forth and weeping, bearing precious seed, shall doubtless come again with rejoicing, bringing his sheaves with him."* The psalmist describes the seed as *"precious,"* but it also seems to indicate a promise to those who weep over lost souls. Does it mean that if we weep, we will with certainty win those lost souls we weep for?

Here is what C.H. Spurgeon said on the subject.

> *"Though I can understand the possibility of an earnest sower never reaping, I cannot understand the possibility of an earnest sower being content not to reap. I cannot comprehend any one of you Christian people trying to win souls and not having results, and being satisfied without results. I can suppose that you may love the Lord, and may have been trying your best for years unsuccessfully, but then I am sure you feel unhappy about it. I can not only suppose that to be the case, but I am thankful that you are*

unhappy. I hope the unhappiness will increase with you, till at last in anguish of your spirit, you shall cry, like Rachel, 'Give me children or I die! Give me fruits or I cannot live!' Then you will be the very person described in the text: you go forth weeping, bearing seed that is precious to you; and you must have results, you must come again rejoicing, bringing your sheaves with you."

May the Lord help us to get a burden for sinners and souls that are all around us, dying every day without Christ and heading for an eternity without hope. Perhaps the reason why we don't see more souls coming to know the Savior is because we have dry eyes and little concern. May we take seriously their soul's condition and not be careless and haphazard with such eternal consequences.

When I begin to plant my garden, I like to begin with fresh seed. It just feels better to start with new seed for the new season. Unless, you have properly stored previous unused seeds in a proper place and temperature, those seeds begin to lose their effectiveness and their ability to germinate.

What is germination? The dictionary defines the word germinate this way: *"to come into being, to begin to grow."*

I found out one year the hard way about this thing of germination. I unknowingly planted a bag of seed that was one year old, and that had evidently not been properly stored. I planted them and, with eager anticipation, waited for the sprouts to appear. After a couple of weeks, there wasn't much happening. It had been long enough time for them to begin to grow, but only a few seeds sprouted here and there. Thinking that maybe the birds found them or maybe they just weren't put in the ground at the proper depth, I replanted the same seeds again. Another two weeks passed, and still nothing doing. Now I'm getting frustrated. I'm losing a great deal of time, not to mention the extra amount of time and work. I'm also now getting very curious. What is going on here? I have not experienced this problem before. I checked the seed bag again and then I realized that it was old seed. After researching, I found out that yes, old seed loses its ability to germinate, to begin the process of coming into being and growing. The seed had been in the bag too long. The only way for the seed to be effective is for it to simply get out of the bag and into the ground. It has to be planted in the soil so that it can come into being and begin to grow.

Spiritually speaking, we must get the seed out of the bag! If we don't get the seed of God's Word out, it will not have the chance to be put into the heart of man, where it can come into being and grow. If we keep it to ourselves, it won't help anyone; it won't bear fruit or produce. We must get the seed out of the bag. We have been given the great commission to tell the good news, to spread the gospel everywhere we go, and to let the whole world know. This seed is powerful, but it must be shared. Don't keep it to yourself. Get the seed out of the bag!

Chapter 4
The Sacrifice of the Seed

Every time I go out to the garden to plant seeds, I never cease to be amazed at how one little seed is going to turn into so much more. The corn seed seems to be the most incredible to me. How one kernel of corn, in just two or three months, will turn into a tall stalk that holds several full ears of corn on it that contains hundreds of kernels of each ear of corn. One kernel multiplies into hundreds and hundreds of kernels of corn. It just blows my mind. Yet, the only way that can happen is for that one kernel of corn to die to itself. That one kernel of corn must sacrifice itself, but in so doing, it will bring new life to so many more.

John 12:24, *"Verily, verily, I say unto you, Except a corn of wheat fall into the ground and die, it abideth alone: but if it die, it bringeth forth much fruit."*

I can think of no better illustration of this thought and verse than what was brought out here by Oliver B. Greene.

"Certainly when He referred to corn or a grain of wheat falling into the ground, He used an illustration easily understood by the people to whom He spoke. Every person who heard Him that day knew that a seed laid on a shelf or kept in a jar would never produce fruit! The seed must be put into the ground, it must die, and when the heart of that seed springs into life it will produce a head of wheat with many grains. We must be content to allow the seed to fall into the ground and die if we expect to produce a harvest of wheat. This beautiful figure of the seed and the harvest sets forth a great spiritual truth: JESUS had to die, His death was a divine imperative. The life of the world depended upon the death of the Saviour. He was that 'corn of wheat,' that Seed that must fall into the ground and die. As long as He tabernacled among men in a body of flesh, though sinless, perfect, holy, without spot or blemish, He abode alone. His holiness, His

righteousness, His purity could not save men; those attributes could only show men how unholy and ungodly they were and how badly they needed a Saviour. His death on the cross, His shed blood, was the only way a harvest of souls could be reaped. Unless Jesus, the "corn of wheat," fall into the ground and die, there would be no harvest; but through His death, burial, and resurrection "according to the Scriptures" He would bring forth much fruit. Eternal life for the multitudes of the world depended upon His death. 'Except' is a very strong word as used here. It means there was no other way, it had to be death, 'EXCEPT a corn of wheat fall into the ground, EXCEPT a corn of wheat die, there can BE no harvest!' The sacrificial death of Jesus was the only way salvation could be purchased for Hell-deserving men and women."

Just as the corn seed sacrificed itself for the good of many more, so Jesus died that we might have eternal life. The Bible tells us in John 15:13,

"Greater love hath no man than this, that a man lay down his life for his friends." Jesus laid Himself down that the entire world could be brought back to God. He willingly sacrificed Himself for the good of the multitude. Romans 5:15, *"For if through the offence of one many be dead, much more the grace of God, and by the gift by grace, which is by one man, Jesus Christ, hath abounded unto many."*

When the seed sacrifices itself, it opens up the way for many others to come after it and to spring forth in new life. Laying oneself down is not an easy task, but when we do, it is amazing what can happen because of our sacrifice.

Jesus laid down His life for us because He loved us, and we can lay down ourselves for those around us as well. Not only in giving up our physical life for them, but we can also lay down our time and our own interests for the good and interests of others. Maybe we sacrifice something we have been waiting for and wanting when we see someone else in need or that we can be a help and a blessing to someone else. We out of love, willingly lay down our self for another. The Bible reminds us that there is no greater love than that right there. It is selfless, it is sacrificial and it is Christ-like.

It can be a rather inspiring and also convicting thought and reminder of what God can do with one individual who is willing to give up his own self for the good of others. Inspiring, in the regard that God can take one person's life and transform it and do so much with it. However, convicting in the aspect of if an individual chooses not to lay himself down, how much more is forfeited that will never come to pass.

I think of a missionary who makes the decision to answer the call to the mission field. God begins to burden them and shows them where He wants them to go to spread the gospel. They move their family, perhaps have to learn a new language, leave the comforts of home, and go to a foreign place to tell others of the good news of Christ. They laid themselves down that others might hear of Jesus. By laying themselves down, potentially multitudes can receive salvation. Out of their decision and obedience to sacrifice themselves, many others were brought into life, eternal life in Heaven.

God blesses those who lay themselves down for someone else and gives them fruit to their account in more ways than they could ever imagine. When we put someone else in front of us, God is well pleased. That kind of thinking and attitude is not of the world but only comes from

Christ as He works in us and through us to reach others and to show them the love of Christ.

This is the mind of Christ according to Philippians 2:4, *"Look not every man on his own things, but every man also on the things of others."*

Ask the Lord to give you a heart for others and to look for ways you can lay down yourself for the sake of someone else. It may sound backward, but Jesus taught us and showed us that the way to have life is to die and that by giving, we can gain more than we could ever possibly think. Like that corn seed that gives itself up and ultimately brings in so much more fruit, so God will use and bless our life with more fruit than we could have ever thought possible when we lay down our life for Him and for the gospel.

Lord, help me to lay down my life for the good of others, for little is much when God is in it.

Chapter 5
The Water of Life and the SON-shine

Once the seeds have been planted in the ground, they will soon need a very basic but most vital necessity, which, of course, is water. In order for that seed to be successful, it must have moisture; it must receive water as one of its most critical needs for survival. Without the water, those seeds and your garden will not simply develop as they should. From the beginning of the seed turning into a sprout and continuing on to grow into a plant and ultimately to bear fruit, water is life-giving to it all. When a garden doesn't get the water it so desperately needs, that garden will turn hard, it will turn dry, and your plants will die out.

You will certainly have to keep your eye on the weather forecast to keep track of your opportunity for rain. If there is no rain in sight for any great length of time, you will have to pull out a water hose. You must see to it that your garden stays moist and wet. The longer that garden goes without water, the sooner you will lose your garden growth and your hard work. Water is essential to its growth, and it keeps its root system from drying up. Water is used to transport nutrients and minerals from the soil to the plant. Basically, water keeps it alive and growing. If you want to have a good garden, you will have to have that most important and precious, life-giving water.

The Bible has a lot to say about water. When Jesus met the woman at the well in John 4:7, He saith unto her, *"Give me to drink."* She, understanding that He is a Jew, knows this is unusual for Him to ask that, so she questions Him. Jesus begins to help her understand who He really is and that, honestly, she should be asking Him for water instead. Jesus begins to explain to her that He is the Water of life. Jesus was saying to her that whoever drinks of this water here in the well shall surely thirst again, but he who drinks of the water that He gives shall never thirst again. This water Jesus speaks of here is a picture of salvation. Every human being that has ever been born has a longing down deep in their soul, and it can only be quenched by the Lord Jesus Christ. Psalm 107:9 tells us, *"For he satisfieth the longing soul and filleth the hungry soul with goodness."* Jesus was simply saying, "Lady, I have what you're looking for. I have what you need and can't get anywhere else. I am the living water."

People every day are searching for something to satisfy their thirsty and longing souls. They may turn to all sorts of different things, but Jesus is what they need. Jesus is to the thirsty soul of man what water is to a dry and thirsty garden.

Jesus said in John 7:37, *"If any man thirst, let him come unto me, and drink. He that believeth on me, as the scripture hath said, out of his belly shall flow rivers of living water."* This living water is a type of the Holy Spirit that lives within us that renews and refreshes us and cleanses us day by day.

Water not only gives life, but it also sustains. To keep those plants healthy and strong, they must consistently continue to receive that water. Ephesians 5:26 gives us a picture of water as the Word of God. In order for us as Christians to consistently be healthy and grow, we need to continuously find ourselves soaking and taking in the Word of God. It sustains us, it cleanses us of sin, it feeds our thirsty souls and keeps us nourished in the things of the Lord.

If a garden plant gets no water, soon it will begin to dry up and wilt away. A Christian who neglects the Word of God over a period of time will become dry in his soul. The ground of his heart will become parched and hard. As the garden feeds and draws nourishment from that life giving and sustaining water, so we must continue to feed from and draw from the Word of God. As water is critical to the natural garden, so the water of life is absolutely vital to the health, growth, and nourishment to our souls. The soul that seeks after God shall never dry up. Matthew 5:6 *"Blessed are they which do hunger and thirst after righteousness for they shall be filled."* The Lord delights in those who desire to follow His ways and He will gladly grant them their heart's desire and reward them with bountiful blessings.

Isaiah 58:11 *"And the Lord shall guide thee continually, and satisfy thy soul in drought, and make fat thy bones: and thou shalt be like a watered garden, and like a spring of water, whose waters fail not."*

We simply cannot underestimate the many benefits of this filling, sustaining, life-giving water of the Word of God. Make sure that your garden receives that much-needed water, and let the Lord and His Word quench your thirsty soul.

There is yet another equally important thing that your garden will need, and that is plenty of sunshine. It is highly recommended that when you plant a garden that you do so in an area that can get plenty of sunshine. As much as the garden needs rain or water, it must also have the sun. Your garden needs a great deal of light from the sun each day. A garden that does not get sunlight will die.

The light represents Christ, the Son of God. John 1:4 *"In him was life, and the life was the light of men"* and also in John 1:9, *"That was the true Light, which lighteth every man that cometh into the world."*

When I think of the sunlight in the garden, I think of the Son light of the world, which is Jesus. In John 12:46, Jesus said, *"I am come a light into the world, that whosoever believeth on me should not abide in darkness."* John 8:12, *"Then spake Jesus again unto them, saying, I am the light of the world: he that followeth me shall not walk in darkness, but shall have the light of life."*

God sent His Son into this dark world to give us the light of life. He gave us His Son to die on the cross for our sins and to show us the way. We cannot navigate this life without the light of the world, that is Jesus, leading us, guiding us and showing us the way. We need His power, we need His strength, and we need His presence because without it we would be lost in darkness. Without the light of Christ in our lives, we will spiritually die. Without the light that is in Jesus to shine the way, we will remain lost in our sin.

Just as light is necessary for the life of the garden, likewise is the light of Christ necessary for eternal life.

Sunlight has many other benefits as well according to medical research. According to an article writte by Paul Frysh, *"The sun's UV rays help your body make this nutrient, which is important for your bones, blood cells and immune system. It also helps you take in and use certain minerals, like calcium and phosphorus."*

Moderate amounts of the sun provides a host of health benefits to us, as well as regulating our sleep pattern, and promoting our overall emotional well-being. Many people enjoy the bright early morning sun as they start their day. There's just something about the sun that wakes us up and gets us going as it begins to shine. It gives us that feel of a fresh new day, a new start, a new beginning.

As the light of Jesus shines in our hearts, He gives us new hope, and He gives us new life. He forgives us of our sin, and we start with a fresh, clean slate as a new creature in Christ. (II Corinthians 5:17)

Sunlight is a vital source to plants because of the process of photosynthesis, which converts light energy into chemical energy, which is, in turn, made into food. Without that food, the plants will fail to receive the things they need to live. Neither can a child of God fail to receive the spiritual light that comes from God without suffering the consequences of it. As plants need the natural sun, so we need the Son of God.

Psalm 84:11, *"For the Lord God is a sun and shield: the Lord will give grace and glory: no good thing will he withhold from them that walk uprightly."*

John Gill stated this:

> *"Christ is "the sun of righteousness", and it is in the house of God that he arises upon his people with healing in his wings, Malachi 4:2, he is like the sun, the great light, the fountain of light, the light of the world, that dispels darkness, makes day, and gives light to all the celestial bodies, moon and stars, church and ministers; he is a "sun" to enlighten his people with the light of his grace, to warm them with the beams of his love, to cheer and refresh their souls with the light of his countenance, and to make them fruitful and flourishing..."*

When the light of the Son of God is upon our hearts and lives, He shows us the way, and He gives us the fuel to grow and to bear fruit. We will be spiritually healthy, full of life, and as productive as we should be.

Sometimes, certain ministers will close a service with a phrase that we see in Numbers 6:24-26 that says, *"The Lord bless you and keep you; The Lord make His face shine upon you, And be gracious to you; The Lord lift up His countenance upon you, and give you peace."*

This is referring to the favor and blessing of God being bestowed upon our lives. The truth is, God has blessed every one of us. He has and continues to give us His unmerited and undeserved grace. Yet, I do think that as He looks upon us in our lives, He sees where we are, and He knows our hearts. He sees us when we are truly seeking more of Him and when we are not. He recognizes when we desire to know His ways and His Word deeper, and He gives us an extra measure of favor, blessing, insight, and understanding.

We understand the need and the importance of the sun shining upon our garden because it brings so many life-giving benefits. In order to live the best life that God intends for us to live, we must seek and desire to have the wonderful blessings of having His face shining upon our lives. Without the sun the garden will not grow.

Oh, how important the SON is in our life! If we desire to have the growth, the fruit and the reward, we must also have the SON shine as well!

Chapter 6

The Weeds of Sin

Weeds, weeds, weeds! Oh, those never-ending, stubborn, pesky weeds. One thing is for sure: if you are going to plant a garden, you are going to have to fight against weeds. Before you begin to plant a garden, you had better already have or soon get a reliable, heavy-duty, yet simple tool called a hoe. That hoe will be your best friend, and you will be spending a lot of time with it in your hands. It wouldn't be a bad idea also to get yourself a good pair of gloves to prevent hand sores while you use it too.

You can have your garden clear of weeds before you plant the first seed, but it will not take long before those weeds start popping up everywhere. It is simply amazing how and where they just mysteriously come from. It's like someone raids your garden overnight and secretly plants weed particles that soon appear all over the place.

It reminds me of the story of the wheat and the tares in Matthew 13:24-28. *"Another parable put he forth unto them saying, The kingdom of heaven is likened unto a man which sowed good seed in his field; But while men slept, his enemy came and sowed tares among the wheat, and went his way. But when the blade was sprung up, and brought forth fruit, then appeared the tares also. So the servant of the householder came and said unto him Sir, didst not thou sow good seed in thy field? From whence then hath it tares? He said unto them, An enemy hath done this…"*

The enemy is the devil, and the weeds represent sin. These weeds are like an enemy that will do everything it can, if left alone, to destroy the good plants you have planted. Therefore, you must deal with them. If you do not keep those weeds in check, they will overtake your plants and they will choke them out. Weeds will take away and rob the moisture, sunlight, and all the nutrients your garden plants are living off of. They will literally rob everything around it and suck the life out of your good plants that are growing. We mentioned this earlier as we talked about preparing the soil. Mark 4:7 *"And some fell among thorns, and the thorns grew up, and choked it and it yielded no fruit."* Just as sure as you begin to grow in the Lord, the devil will show up mighty quick and start planting his own weeds of sin right beside you. He will try and tempt you, distract you, and try to hinder and even stop your growth from taking place.

Though you may have removed those weeds at the beginning of planting, they will come back again. The truth is, we will be dealing with and removing weeds from start to finish in our garden.

It is much the same in our life as well. We will be dealing with sin from our first day to our last day on Earth. When the devil tempted Jesus with sin on three different occasions, Jesus resisted. He fought back. Though Jesus defeated the devil each time, the Bible says in Luke 4:13, *"And when the devil had ended all temptation, he departed from him for a season."*

Even though the devil didn't win, he would come back again at another time. Sin is relentless; it just keeps coming back at us, tempting us, enticing us, luring us, and trying to cause us to fall. Therefore, we must be on guard, we must be looking to spot sin when it enters into the garden of our life. I Peter 5:8, *"Be sober, be vigilant, because your adversary the devil, as a roaring lion, walketh about seeking whom he may devour."* As long as we are in this flesh, we will have to contend with sin, but do not despair, for greater is

He that is in us than he that is in this world. We can be overcomers. We can be conquerors through Him that loved us. (Romans 8:37)

When we are removing those weeds in the garden, we must get to the bottom of it, and root it out. You cannot just cut down the weed, it must be cut out, it must be uprooted.

Someone once said that if a person has cancer, you cannot simply talk to it real nice and ask it to go away and make it be gone. You cannot deal lightly with cancer. No, you deal with it aggressively; you must get to the root of it and remove it from the body. The devil doesn't play nice, and he doesn't play fair, so we must be quick to remove the sin once we find it in our lives.

We must fight back against the sin that continues to plague us. Those sins that doth so easily beset us. (Hebrews 12:2) If left unchecked, unconfessed, and undealt with, those weeds of sin will take over. It will get out of hand fast, and they will choke out every bit of good fruit that is growing in our lives.

I have learned the hard way how fast weeds in the garden can take over. There were times that I recognized I needed to spend time removing the weeds in the garden, but for one reason or another, I didn't get to it, and soon it was out of control.

Sometimes, we may recognize that there is sin in our lives, and that is a good start, but if we do not act upon it, it will soon get out of hand. The person who only took a drink here and there never imagined they would become an alcoholic. Sin will take you farther than you wanted to go, keep you longer than you wanted to stay, and cost you a price you never wanted to pay. Weeds and sin act very much the same; they spread, and they multiply. Don't let the weeds in your garden get out of hand, and don't let the weeds of sin get a stronghold in your life, either.

A weed, like sin, is an enemy, and it cannot be left alone. As soon as we find it, we must get rid of it.

How do we get rid of it? First, we confess it before God. We acknowledge it, admit it, and be honest with ourselves before God. Second, we ask for His help in resisting it. James 4:7 tells us, *"...Resist the devil, and he will flee from you."* Third, we can use the Word of God. Each time that the devil tempted Jesus, Jesus quoted the scripture back to him. Jesus said, *"It is written," "It is written,"* and *"It is said."* Jesus gave us the blueprint and the example of how to resist and defeat the devil. He used the Word of God. God has given us a weapon, but it is up to us to use the sword of God's Word to fight off the devil and those weeds of sin.

This is also where daily discipline comes into play. If I do not spend regular time watching out for those weeds that pop up, soon the garden can become a huge mess. Likewise, if I do not spend regular daily time guarding my heart, spending time with the Lord, and repenting of sin, my life can turn into a big mess fast. The Lord has given us the Holy Spirit to call us out, to convict, and to chasten us (Hebrews 12:6) when we have sin in our life. That is when we must humbly bring our sin to the Lord and ask for forgiveness and mercy. I John 1:9 *"If we confess our sin, he is faithful and just to forgive us our sin, and to cleanse us from all unrighteousness."* As we acknowledge and confess our sin, the Lord helps us to pull those weeds out of our lives in order to keep the soil of our hearts clean and weed-free.

Putting in the time and effort into faithfully pulling the weeds of your garden and also the weeds in your life will be worth the effort in the end when you see the difference that it can make. Don't give up; stay on top of those weeds, and you will be glad you did.

Chapter 7
The Growing Garden

Watching your garden grow is one of the most exciting things about a garden. Watching everything emerge from the ground, and watching it expand from a little sprout to a full-fledged plant with fruit on it is amazing. It is just neat to watch these plants transforming right before your eyes and knowing you are having a part to play in it all. It can be challenging but also very satisfying as you see it all unfold and bloom right in your garden.

Growth is exciting. Kids love to watch even their own growth. They enjoy taking a pencil and marking their height on a wall or door, then standing there and checking it again the next time to see if they got taller. We love to measure and see our growth. It doesn't always happen fast, but slowly and surely, growth does take place if all the conditions for growing are right.

Growth should be natural. If there is no growth happening, something is wrong somewhere. A baby that is born doesn't stay a baby forever. As much as mom and dad might like for it to stay little, babies grow up. If the baby doesn't grow properly, they take it to the doctor so they can determine what the problem is and try to find a way to fix it.

If your garden plants are not growing, something isn't right and it needs to be looked into to see what the problem is. When the proper time has been given, and all the conditions of the garden are right, growth should naturally be taking place.

Not only is growth natural, growth is expected. As a child is born, before long, it gets bigger, stronger, and starts developing more and more. They will soon learn how to walk and talk, run, and do cartwheels in the coming years. They will continue growing through the years until they mature and reach adulthood.

The Bible teaches us this same idea in I Peter 2:2, *"As newborn babes, desire the sincere milk of the word, that ye may grow thereby."* A newborn naturally desires milk from its mother and then later in a bottle. The milk helps it to get all the vitamins, minerals and nutrients it needs to grow. However, as it gets older, there comes a time for that baby to graduate from the milk to more solid things and ultimately be able to eat meat as it gets older.

The apostle Paul, in his letter to the Corinthians, said in 1 Corinthians 3:1-3, *"And, I brethren could not speak unto you as unto spiritual, but as unto carnal, even as unto babes in Christ. I have fed you with milk, and not with meat: for hitherto ye were not able to bear it, neither yet now are ye able. For ye are yet carnal..."*

At this point in their spiritual life, they had been given more than enough time to have grown and developed into deeper, stronger things of the Lord. However, they had failed to mature in the Lord. They were still as newborn babes in the Lord. When they ought to have been teaching the Word of God, they were still needing to be taught themselves. Hebrews 5:12 *"For when for the time ye ought to be teachers, ye have need that one teach you again which be the first principles of the oracles of God; and are become such as have need of milk, and not of strong meat."* They were childish, carnal, and they were being rebuked for their failure in maturing and growing up in the faith. Their lack of development was a problem that needed to be addressed. Paul is saying, "It is time for you to put away childish things, and it is past time for you to grow up."

67

The Corinthians were more concerned with the messenger rather than the message. While some claimed they were following the teachings of Paul, others were claiming to follow the teachings of Apollos and it had caused contention among the believers. I Corinthians 3:3-5, *"For ye are yet carnal: for whereas there is among you envying, and strife, and divisions, are ye not carnal, and walk as men? For while one saith, I am of Paul; and another, I am of Apollos; are ye not carnal? Who then is Paul, and who is Apollos, but ministers by whom ye believed, even as the Lord gave to every man."* Paul calls them out and says, "Hey, you are all missing it. This isn't about following a minister; this is about following Christ. Let's not get so caught up on the messenger, more than the message from God."

Paul simply reminds them that they, as ministers, are only doing their small part to proclaim the gospel, but it is Christ who makes the difference in the hearts of men. I Corinthians 3:6, *"I have planted, Apollos watered; but God gave the increase. So then neither is he that planteth any thing, neither he that watereth; but God that giveth the increase. Now he that planteth and he that watereth are one; and every man shall receive his own reward according to his own labour."*

H.A. Ironside said, *"The servant has no power to cause the Word to produce fruit. The servant is nothing, but God is everything."* Just as we plant the seed in our garden, we step back and wait to see what comes of it. We cannot force the seed to grow, but nature must take over and run its course. Neither can we force the seed of God's Word to produce in the heart of man. Our job is to simply plant the seed and let God do the work from there.

We all have our part to play, and we are not to be in some kind of competition with one another. We are ultimately working toward the same goal and the same cause to see others come to know the Lord as their personal Savior. One minister may plant the seed of God's Word, and another minister may soften and encourage that seed that has been planted by another, but it is God who gives life to that seed. Paul and Apollos were not rivals in the ministry; they were on the same team to point others to Jesus, and neither should we be rivals today. Neither should we puff one minister up over another, for as Paul reminds us, we are to be one in Christ. If we just humbly and faithfully do our part to plant the seed and water that seed, God will take care of the results. God will reward His laborers according to their work for Him in His field.

We must remember that before there can be growth, there first must be something planted in the ground, so let's not fail to plant the seed so that growth can start to take place. If there's no seed, you can be sure there will be no growth.

As we mentioned earlier, growth is expected. II Peter 3:18, *"But grow in grace, and in the knowledge of our Lord and Savior Jesus Christ…"*

This verse gives us a command and an expectation to grow. If we are not growing, and if we are not maturing and developing in the things of the Lord, then something is failing somewhere, and we will bear no fruit. Our spiritual life should be one that shows progress and growth. One of the ways we do that is by growing in our knowledge of the Lord. How do we do that? By learning more about Him, by reading His Word, by listening to good preaching, by listening to fellow believers who are strong in the Lord and can help us learn more about Him and understand more of Him. Yet, at some point, we should be able to teach the same to those who come after us. The burden is upon us to spend time learning about the Lord, whether through time in Scripture or by life experience with God. If we are not growing, we are not obeying God or fulfilling His purpose for our lives.

The whole purpose of the farmer planting a garden is to ultimately reap fruit out of that garden. If the plant is bearing no fruit, it is pointless; it is a waste of time. We don't put all the time, work, and investment into the garden to get nothing out of it.

Likewise, God intends and expects us as a child of God to grow and to bear fruit, and if we do not do that, then we are unprofitable to Him, and we are not fulfilling His desire for us. When we fail to grow and bear fruit, that is when we may be in danger of being punished, chastised, or even cut down. John 15:2 *"Every branch in me that beareth not fruit he taketh away…"* This matter of growing in the Lord, growing in our faith, and bearing fruit and evidence of it is serious business, and we need not take it lightly.

John 15:1-5 says that we should bear fruit, more fruit and much fruit.

We are not here to live for ourselves. If we have been born again and have become a follower of Christ, we should be living for Him and not for our self.

Jesus was no exception. He also had a time of growth and development as well.

Luke 2:52, *"And Jesus increased in wisdom and stature and in favour with God and man."* Though He was one hundred percent God in the flesh, He was also one hundred percent man

71

and took on the full experience of growing up like any other person did. He, as a man, familiarized himself with the laws and customs and learned things as any other man, and He became a teacher of others, so much that they were amazed at what all He knew (Mark 6:2-3). Jesus grew, developed, and bore much fruit, and He obeyed His Father's will.

I would also like to mention another helpful thing in aiding the growth of your garden, and that is fertilizer. Fertilizer can give plants an extra boost of nutrients, like a vitamin. It promotes good health and makes the plant grow bigger, better, and stronger. Fertilizer helps to enrich the soil.

I like to think of fertilizer as those people who come alongside us to help encourage our walk with the Lord. This is why it is so important to find ourselves at the house of God, fellowshipping with the people of God. These fellow believers are like fertilizer in our spiritual life. They promote us to stay strong in the Lord. They can pray with us, encourage us, and give us extra support. We all need some extra encouragement from time to time. Perhaps you are going through a difficult time, and you get a call, a card, or a visit from a loving brother or sister in the Lord. Maybe they put their arm around you at church and let you know that they are praying for you. My, what a boost it can give you to strengthen you in your faith. The Lord knows what we are going through, and at just the right time we need it, He sends somebody by our way to fertilize us with some encouragement. Perhaps the Lord wants to use you to encourage and fertilize someone else's faith.

God is very much interested in our growth. At the beginning of the church in Acts 2, Peter and the disciples began to preach, and they were filled with the Holy Ghost, and they began to speak in other known languages. The people were amazed at what was happening as the power of God fell that day, and many believed on the Lord as a result. The Bible tells us in Acts 2:41, *"And the same day there were added unto them about three thousand souls."* The church grew that day, but it didn't stop there. Those new believers got on fire for God, got united with one another, and started helping and taking care of one another. They began to pray and meet together to learn about Jesus and encourage one another, and they kept on growing and adding to the church. Acts 2:46-47 *"And they, continuing daily with one accord in the temple, and breaking bread from house to house, did eat their meat with gladness and singleness of heart, Praising God, and having favour with all the people. And the*

73

Lord added to the church daily such as should be saved."

This was a group of believers that was growing in their faith and in their church.

Just as the farmer intends and expects his garden to grow, so the Lord expects and intends for us to grow and increase our faith. As the children's song simply puts it, "Read your Bible, pray every day, pray every day, pray every day, read your Bible pray every day, and you'll GROW, GROW, GROW!

Get in the Word, get on your knees, and get in the house of God with the saints of God and let your spiritual garden grow and bear fruit, more fruit, yea much fruit, for the glory of God.

Chapter 8
The Protection of the Garden

When it comes to my garden, I have to begin with this question in mind. How do I plan to defend it? What plan will I have to protect it? If I do not have an adequate way to keep it safe, I will soon be working for nothing. You see, in my case, I live in a rural country area with pastures and woods. The wildlife is a constant problem to deal with. There have been several times that the deer and other critters have gotten into my garden and have helped themselves to all that was growing in it. All that time I have invested in tilling, planting, watering, fertilizing, and watching it grow can all be lost in a very short time if I do not have a good plan to keep out the wildlife or the intruders that seek to eat up all the fruit I have earnestly worked for. Keeping your garden safe from predators is crucial. No one wants to spend all that time, energy, and money to watch it all be destroyed. It is disheartening to see it happen. Therefore, you must do whatever it takes to protect it at all costs.

Just as those weeds from within the garden soil seek to choke out and cut off the plants from growing and developing, there are also enemies from the outside that will do all they can to get in our spiritual garden to destroy us as well.

The world, the flesh, and the devil are enemies against the child of God. The world system seeks to entice us, to lure us into sin. It invites and tempts us to do whatever we want to do or whatever feels good. Live in the moment and do what pleases you. It is a mindset and philosophy that is selfish, carnal, wicked and anti-God. This is an enemy that seeks to destroy your walk and relationship with God. It is an attempt to undermine and cut off your spiritual growth, and its ultimate end is to leave you fruitless and barren. It is a subtle enemy; it makes it appeal to our flesh, and it sounds so good to the flesh.

This enemy, like the serpent in the Garden of Eden, tempted and caused doubt upon what God had said and tricked Eve into thinking that God was withholding some wonderful thing from her. The truth is God was trying to protect her from something very awful called sin, but the enemy who opposed God and His plan fooled and tricked her into falling for it. The enemy wants to destroy the beautiful and wonderful work that God is doing in your life. Just as we have become so invested in our garden, so God has invested everything in us.

The last thing any farmer wants is for that garden that he has worked so hard in to be destroyed. Neither does God want to see the enemy get into our lives, get into our hearts, get into our minds, and corrupt and devour the work that is taking place in our life with Him.

This is why we must defend it. This is why we must guard against the enemy gaining access. The enemy doesn't play nice, nor does he play fair; the enemy plays for keeps. The Bible tells us in John 10:10, *"The thief cometh not, but for to steal, and to kill, and to destroy. I am come that they might have life, and that they might have it more abundantly."* Whether it is weeds, wildlife, or the wicked one, their goal is all the same. Steal the fruit, take it away, devour it, and kill the good work of that garden.

I Peter 5:8 also shows us more about this enemy we fight against. *"Be sober, be vigilant; because your adversary the devil, as a roaring lion, walketh about, seeking whom he may devour."*

As the wildlife discovers your garden, it begins looking for a way to get in and get what it is after. If your garden is protected by one of various means of protection, it stands a much better chance of surviving. However, if that garden has no means of protection, then it is very susceptible to the enemy getting in and helping itself. The Bible says, be alert, be on guard, be aware, be on the lookout for the enemy. Be watchful against the enemy as it seeks to gain entry into your heart, mind, and life. As that enemy in the wildlife looks for a way to get in your garden, so the devil is looking for a way to get to us. He is looking for that one area that maybe is a weakness, that one area that may be more easily accessible, and if he finds it, he will pounce on it.

As we must protect our garden, we must also protect our heart. Proverbs 4:23 directs us to *"Keep thy heart with all diligence; for out of it are the issues of life."* The word *keep* here means to guard, to protect, to defend. There are some things that we need to guard and protect at all costs. We must protect and guard our heart, our spirit, our inner man, our very core. Imagine what damage can be done to a heart where things such as bitterness, anger, jealousy, lust, and pride gain access. The devil tries to corrupt and contaminate our hearts. He may whisper lies in our minds, or perhaps he tries to plant seeds of envy in our hearts, whichever is the easiest route to get into our heart. Protecting our heart, like protecting our garden, is key. That's why the verse continues on by saying that we should guard our heart *"with all diligence."*

To do our very best, to spare no effort or no expense. You cannot be too careful. I like to think of a gatekeeper who keeps the city or a person who sits in the guardhouse at an entrance. This person is designed to ensure that anyone who does not have the proper credentials or permission to enter is kept out. Their job is to keep the gate, to protect the property, and to keep the unpermitted person from gaining access inside. The gatekeeper has a great responsibility to protect and keep safe what's inside the gate.

What are the gates in our lives? The gates can be our eyes and the things we allow ourselves to see. The gates can be our ears and what we permit them to hear and to take in our minds: the music we listen to, which has a dwelling place in our minds, and the worldly voices around us. The gates can be our mouth and the words that we say, for they are an indication of what is in our heart already. Matthew 12:34, *"...for out of the abundance of the heart the mouth speaketh."* The heart is at the center of it all, therefore we must fight to keep it safe, pure, undefiled, and clean before God.

We are the gatekeeper of our heart, and we have the strong responsibility of protecting and keeping it safe from the enemy. This is why it is so important that we keep out the wrong influences, and keep away the voices that seek to go contrary to the ways of God. We must keep away from our eyes those things that only tempt us and lure us to sinful things, just as the psalmist said in Psalm 101:3, *"I will set no wicked thing before mine eyes…"* We cannot underestimate the seriousness, the importance, and the utmost responsibility we have to protect our own heart.

How, then, do we go about protecting our heart? Ephesians 6:11-17 answers that for us.

"Put on the whole armour of God, that ye may be able to stand against the wiles of the devil. For we wrestle not against flesh and blood, but against principalities, against powers, against the rulers of the darkness of this world, against spiritual wickedness in high places. Wherefore take unto you the whole armour of God, that ye may be able to withstand in the evil day, and having done all, to stand. Stand therefore, having your loins girt about with truth, and having on the breastplate of righteousness; And your feet shod with the preparation of the gospel of peace; Above all, taking the shield of faith, wherewith ye shall be able to quench all the fiery darts of the wicked. And take the helmet of salvation, and the sword of the Spirit, which is the word of God: Praying always with all prayer and supplication in the Spirit, and watching thereunto with all perseverance and supplication for all saints;"

Albert Barnes commented,

"The idea here is, that Satan does not carry on an open warfare. He does not meet the Christian soldier face to face. He advances covertly; makes his approaches in darkness; employs cunning rather than power, and seeks rather to delude and betray than to vanquish by mere force. Hence, the necessity of being constantly armed to meet him whenever the attack is made. A man who has to contend with a visible enemy, may feel safe if he only prepares to meet him in the open field. But far different is the case if the enemy is invisible; if he steals upon us slyly and stealthily; if he practices war only by ambushes and by surprises. Such is the foe that we have to contend with - and almost all the Christian struggle is a warfare against stratagems and wiles. Satan does not openly appear. He approaches us not in repulsive forms, but comes to recommend some plausible doctrine, to lay before us some

temptation that shall not immediately repel us. He presents the world in an alluring aspect; invites us to pleasures that seem to be harmless, and leads us in indulgence until we have gone so far that we cannot retreat."

God has given us the weaponry, the tools and the protection we need to not only defend ourselves but to fight against the enemy. He has given us His Word, He has given us His Spirit, He has given us faith and truth, as well as the weapon of prayer. We can arm ourselves with these things to stand against the devil and to watch for his attacks against us as children of God. God has not left us vulnerable, but He has armed us, He has given us the means to protect our hearts and our walk with Him, but we must employ them, or they will be of no use to us.

Just as a defenseless garden is open to the prey, so is our heart if we neglect to protect it with these things God has given us. As you protect your garden, protect your heart as well, for out of it are the issues of life. We have invested too much time, work, sweat, and energy to let the predator steal our hard work in the garden to let it all be taken away and devoured.

I think we could also see another analogy and picture here, that of parenthood. How so? A farmer is there from the time that seed is first planted and watches it grow into a sprout and he faithfully and tenderly cares for and nourishes that life that is growing all the way until it is fully grown and bearing fruit on its own. He makes sure it gets all that it needs and puts it in the best situation for growth to happen and he protects us, fertilizes it, and sees it all the way through.

Similarly, a mom and a dad are there with that little one from the time it is a tiny baby. They watch it grow, they nourish it, take good care of it, and place it in the best environment they can get it in. They teach it, they protect it from harmful influences, and give that growing and maturing child all it needs to grow and develop into a fruitful human being.

They have too much interest, time, energy, and work into developing that person for some outsider to come in and steal it all away and destroy years of diligent efforts. Therefore, protect your investment. It is too valuable to let it all slip away. Whether it is your garden, the garden of your heart, or even someone you have poured your heart into, do not allow the devil or any other enemy to come in and devour the good work that has been done or that God is doing in your heart. Protect it at all costs!

Chapter 9
The Rewarding Harvest

After months of hard work in your garden, there is nothing more satisfying and exciting than to go picking the fruit from your garden. I look forward to the day that I get to "take a bag" to the garden. It is the day I look forward to from the very first day I start working the garden for the new season. It is the prize and reward of all the time, hard work and sweat that has gone into it. I like to have what I call "harvest supper" one night after I have gathered in all the fruits and veggies. This even has a Biblical reference, according to Exodus 23:16. *"And the feast of harvest, the firstfruits of thy labours, which thou hast sown in the field: and the feast of ingathering, which is in the end of the year, when thou hast gathered in thy labours out of the field."* A supper where everything on my plate comes from the garden is an amazing thing. I can eat corn, green beans, squash, carrots, baked potatoes, watermelon and cantaloupe, etc. It is also a great opportunity to reinforce to your kids that in days gone by, if you didn't grow your food, you might not eat, and how important farmers are still to us today for many of our foods.

Could you just go to the store and buy whatever you want without all the trouble and time? Certainly, but there's nothing more enjoyable than eating food that you grew in your very own backyard. You took on the challenge of taking a tiny seed, planting it in good soil, caring for it, protecting it, watching it grow, and then enjoying the fruit of it. Plus, all along the way, you have learned and gained more experience and life lessons from your time tending to the garden. If you have stayed at work in your garden there will be a rewarding harvest at the end.

Galatians 6:9, *"And let us not be weary in well doing: for in due season we shall reap, if we faint not."*

We must not give up, get discouraged, or quit. The harvest takes time. It may take more time than we want it to, but if we stay with it, stay diligent, and be patient, the fruit will come. James 5:7 *"Be patient therefore, brethren, unto the coming of the Lord. Behold, the husbandman waiteth for the precious fruit of the earth, and hath long patience for it, until he receive the early and latter rain."*

"The farmer waits patiently for the grain to grow. It requires

86

time to mature the crop, and he does not become impatient. The idea seems to be, that we should wait for things to develop themselves in their proper season, and should not be impatient before that season arrives. In due time we may expect the harvest to be ripened. We cannot hasten it. We cannot control the rain, the sun, the season; and the farmer therefore patiently waits until in the regular course of events he has a harvest. So we cannot control and hasten the events which are in God's own keeping; and we should patiently wait for the developments of his will, and the arrangements of his providence, by which we may obtain what we desire." Albert Barnes

When I plant my garden, I also like to save a place for the kids to have a little garden of their own as well. They get to choose whatever they want to plant in their garden area and they get to watch it grow, take care of it, and pick the fruit. It's a way to teach them about gardening and how they can see things grow right before their eyes and

87

perhaps get them to be interested in gardening as they get older.

As you can expect with a youngster, they have a hard time waiting for it all to happen. They will plant the seed, and within a day or two, they are checking the ground to see if it has come up yet. Of course, we remind them that these things take time and that it will take a while for it to be ready. It's not so different from us as adults; we, too, like to see instant results with things. The reality, though, is that it just takes time, and a garden is one thing that can be used to teach us patience. We can't hurry it up and make it happen faster; we just have to wait.

Patience tends to be a more and more unpopular thing in the world today. We want instant gratification here and now. We want our fast food, our instant grits, and our overnight packages. We don't like to wait, but there are certain things that you just have to wait for.

We may be witnessing to someone, inviting them to church, and in our minds, we hope they will come to church the next Sunday and give their life to Christ. I'm not saying that can't happen, and I'm sure it does in some situations, but many times that seed that we are planting in others just takes time to develop and to grow. We have to encourage the seed that has been sown and give it tender care and love and allow that seed to grow over time, and as you build a relationship with those people, it has a better chance of bearing fruit in time.

Even for those who have already come to know the Lord, growth takes time. Growth is really a lifetime process. I have heard the saying, "It's not the destination; it's the journey." Along the journey, we have ups and downs, peaks and valleys, bumps and bruises, but as long as we keep moving, we are still headed in the right direction. We are still growing and gaining wisdom and experience from life's situations and circumstances. We are learning about God's faithfulness and love for us in spite of all the times we fell down, but He helped us back up and we gained something from that time. Growth doesn't happen overnight for the garden, nor in our spiritual life either. It just takes time.

A preacher once said, start off with at least fifteen minutes a day reading your Bible and fifteen minutes a day in prayer, and you will begin to grow in the Lord. From there, expand upon it and spend more time with Him each and every day, and you will grow and mature more and more. As we spend more time in His word and yielding ourselves to His Spirit, the more we mature, develop, and bear fruit in our life and for the glory of God.

I'm also convinced that there will be a great number of seeds that we have helped to sow that we may never see the harvest of in this life, but only in the life to come in Heaven. For example, if you laid down a gospel tract somewhere in public and someone picked it up, took it with them, read it, and gave their heart to Christ, we would likely never know about it. We would have no idea who that person was that we planted that seed in, but God does. God saw you lay that seed down, and God saw the one who picked it up, and He began to work in their heart. Though each person had no idea of each other, God knows. Then, one day in Heaven, those two individuals are brought together, and it is told to them what happened, how we were involved in that person accepting Christ and what a rejoicing time it would be for each other! Perhaps the financial offering that you gave to a missionary for his work to spread the gospel that God used to reach others. Maybe it is buying someone a Bible so they could read God's Word for themselves, and then somewhere down the line, they called out unto the Lord in salvation.

There are just too many ways and too many seeds that can be sown that we may not ever see the results of in this life, but you can be sure that God is keeping a record of it all, and it will be made known to us in eternity. So keep planting those seeds, and don't give up, don't get discouraged, for the harvest truly is plenteous, and the fields are white unto harvest. So as the old song asked, "Who will go and work for me today?"

The Bible likens the garden or the field to the world. Matthew 13:38, *"The field is the world..."*

Inside that field are workers and laborers, which is you and me. We are working the field; we are working the world, planting and sowing and nurturing the seed of God's Word, looking for the day when we can reap the harvest or bring souls to Jesus. All the work that we do in that field will surely be worth it. Yes, it is a challenging work, a tiring work, but it is also a rewarding work that we must not give up on.

There is a world of souls out there that need to hear the gospel, that needs someone to sow a seed into their life of Jesus Christ and to tell them of the good news of God's saving grace.

Jesus said in John 4:35, *"Say not ye, There are yet four months and then cometh the harvest? Behold, I say unto you, Lift up your eyes, and look on the fields; for they are white already unto harvest."* Jesus simply says that souls are ready to be brought in; they are out there like ripe fruit ready to be plucked off the vine. All we have to do is look for it, open up our eyes and see the world, see the need. This is the heart cry of Jesus; this is why He came to help save the people from their sins. He told his followers in Luke 10:2, *"Therefore he said unto them, The harvest truly is great, but the labourers are few: pray ye therefore the Lord of the harvest, that he would send forth labourers into his harvest."*

The great commandment and the great commission that Christ has given us is to *"go ye into all the world and preach the gospel to every creature."* Mark 16:15

Everywhere we go, spread the gospel. If it is across the street or across the world, preach the gospel. There can be no harvest if there is no one to claim it. Imagine the folly of a garden being raised and the plants bearing fruit, for it to just hang on the vine too long, decay, rot, and go bad.

What a tragedy it is when the world is filled with souls that are ready to come to Christ, but there are too few doing the work to harvest them or to bring them in. This is why we must respond when the Holy Spirit nudges us to witness to someone, to give them a gospel tract, to show them love and to show them Christ. That they may see the hope that is in us and the changed life that God has brought about in us and that they may see our life in Him and be drawn to the Savior.

How many times have we walked away from someone and missed an opportunity who may have been hurting and needing someone to care, someone to talk to, someone to invite them to know of Christ just when they may have been open and receptive to hear it? May we take it seriously when God speaks to our heart to minister to someone, for we never know the impact that it could make. May we take it with utmost seriousness when we feel God speaking to us about sharing the gospel with others at home and abroad. The world needs Jesus, the world is ready unto harvest, and let us not allow opportunities to pass us by and for those hungry and longing souls to be lost forever because of our negligence and disobedience to the voice of God.

The reason the Lord has not returned yet is that there is still a work to do. He is still giving grace; He is still giving time for the souls of men and women, boys and girls, to come to know Him as their Lord and Saviour. God is with all long-suffering, patiently waiting for you and for me as His servants, His laborers, to sow the seed of the gospel that others may receive it and begin their life in Christ. One day soon, when the final soul is saved, He will say unto His Son, "Go and get my children, and bring them home to live with me forever."

We must be about His business. Do not quit, do not get disheartened, keep the faith, press on, for there is a harvest ripe and ready to claim. When God, like the farmer, comes to claim His great harvest of souls, what joy, what excitement, and what a rewarding time in Heaven it will be!

Chapter 10
The Spiritual Garden

Whether or not you have an actual garden in your yard, the truth is that every one of us has a spiritual garden. How you handle that garden and what results you get out of it depends largely on what you do with it. Our life is like a garden, and what we allow to grow in it makes all the difference in the world.

We must first take a look and see what is the condition of the soil in our heart? Is our heart hard? Is it cold, calloused, stubborn, unconcerned, or apathetic? Is it dry? Hebrews 3:15 tells us *"To day if ye will hear his voice, harden not your hearts..."* Can we hear the voice of God, or are we resistant to it? There is yet hope for a hard heart, for God is able to change our heart as we see in Ezekiel 36:26, *"A new heart also will I give you, and a new spirit will I put within you: and I will take away the stony heart out of your flesh, and I will give you an heart of flesh."* We can begin to pray unto the Lord that He will soften our hearts and help us to be receptive to His Word and His voice as He speaks into our hearts and lives.

We must ensure that our heart is soft and tender so that we will have fertile ground and good soil to work with. By making sure that we seek to have a clean and clear heart before God, as the psalmist said in Psalms 51:10, when he said, *"Create in me a clean heart, O God; and renew a right spirit within me."* As garden soil needs to be clean and clear of debris, so our heart needs to be purified from sin as soon as the Holy Spirit reveals sin in our heart. The soil of this earth will do all it can to pollute our heart and so we must maintain the soil of our heart and keep out the trash and impurities of the world as best we can.

We must then consider the type of seed that we are planting in our life. Is it good seed? Is it the seed of God's Word, or is it corruptible seed? I Peter 1:23, *"Being born again, not of corruptible seed, but of incorruptible, by the Word of God, which liveth and abideth forever."* When we are born physically, we are born in sin. Psalm 51:5, *"Behold, I was shapen in iniquity; and in sin did my mother conceive me."* Our seed is sinful, it is corrupt, and it will decay and die, therefore we must be born again, born by the Spirit of God from above by calling unto Him in repentance and seeking salvation through Christ. His seed is incorruptible; it liveth and abideth forever. The body of a man will deteriorate and die, but our spirit will live on. We must receive this incorruptible seed of God's Word to have eternal life in Heaven. He must make us alive in Christ. Ephesians 2:1, *"And you hath he quickened, who were dead in trespasses and sins."* After we have received His Spirit and His Word, continue to plant and sow His seed into your heart.

The more we plant that seed in our hearts, the more we will see good and godly things grow into fruition in our own lives. Ensure that the seed you are sowing is good seed.

Remember as the seed in the ground dies to itself, so we are called upon to die to ourselves as well. The apostle Paul said, *"I die daily"* in I Corinthians 15:31, and Luke 9:23 instructs us that, *"If any man will come after Me, let him deny himself and take up his cross daily, and follow Me."* Every day is a battle between the flesh and the spirit. Though we have been born again and have Christ living in us, we still have to contend with that old sinful nature inside of us. Yet we now have the power of God inside us to help fight off those sinful ways if we will deny ourselves and yield to Him and follow Him. When we are also willing to lay ourselves down and sacrifice ourselves for the good of others, we may not know just how much more of an impact it could be to others.

Make sure that your heart and life, your spiritual garden, receives the consistent replenishment and nourishment it needs. Keep close to God and allow Him to feed your soul, and always have a thirsty soul for He is truly the only one who can fill us and feed us. Psalm 107:9 *"For He satisfieth the longing soul, and filleth the hungry soul with goodness."* Plant yourself close to the source of the water of His Word, and we will prosper and be fruitful. (Psalm 1:3)

Never neglect your spiritual garden, but make sure that you maintain it and keep out those never ending weeds, those sins that continuously creep up in our life, trying to take hold and ruin the good fruit. When I ride by someone's garden going down the road, it's pretty easy to tell who is keeping up with it and who is not. If it is nice and neat, that means that someone has been diligently working in their garden to keep it weed-free. You can also tell who has not been in their garden for a while because it is all grown over and filled with weeds. Keeping the weeds out is as critical as anything you do in a garden, and so it is critical in our own hearts and lives as well. The longer we neglect our spiritual garden, the less time we spend in God's Word, the less time we are in prayer and in the things of God, the more sin takes up residence in our hearts. That is why we must be watchful for the weeds of sin and kick them out of our garden. Ask the Lord to help you identify sin that needs to be confessed and dealt with.

When you enjoy sweet fellowship with that saint of God who loves the Lord and faithfully serves Him, that is a sign of someone who is spending a great deal of time with the Lord and is taking good care of their spiritual garden and that it is being well maintained.

Your spiritual garden must be a place where growth is happening. Little by little, inch by inch, the goal is to see development and steady growth taking place. Our spiritual life may have ups and downs, setbacks and obstacles to overcome, but overall, it should still be moving forward and growing. We are to keep making gains in every season of our life to be more like Christ.

Paul, writing in Galatians 4:19, said, *"My little children, of whom I travail in birth again until Christ be formed in you."* As a child forms in its mother's womb and grows and develops, so we should be continuing to develop in and through our life with God. That mother goes through many pains and uncomfortable stages, but she is willing to do so as she looks forward to that child that is being formed and created in her womb. Soon, though, she will lay her eyes on and lovingly hold in her arms that precious newborn babe.

Christ is trying to do a work in our hearts and in our lives, and the process may be difficult and hard at times, but we must press on until Christ be formed in us. How long do we keep striving? Ephesians 4:13 tells us, *"Till we all come in the unity of the faith, and of the knowledge of the Son of God, unto a perfect man, unto the measure of the stature of the fullness of Christ."* Keep striving, keep growing, and keep maturing in the Lord as we continue reaching forth and growing toward the mark of Christ-likeness.

As you are growing in Christ, be sure to protect and guard your testimony. The devil seeks to trip us up and to cause us to fall. Therefore, we must constantly watch for his devices against us (II Corinthians. 2:11) and to keep out those harmful forces and worldly influences that desire to hinder or destroy the progress we are making. Just as the serpent found his way in the garden of Eden to tempt Eve, so he wants to tempt and deceive you and me. Fight back, and fight off the enemies, not in your own strength, but in the strength and in the power of the Word of God. Resist him, and he will flee from you. But be ready because he will come back again soon with another trick. He is slick, he is subtle, he is smart, and he knows our weaknesses. Protect the garden of your heart with the utmost earnestness and vigilance. Fill your heart and mind with the weapon of God's Word that you may stand against the devil in the day of battle.

A garden takes hard work, it takes time, it takes diligence and consistency. It's no different in our own life. If we want our spiritual garden to turn out well, we must also work on it. It doesn't just happen. No gardener just scatters some seeds around on the ground and walks away and expects it to work and bring him fruit in the months ahead. No, it takes thoughtful, intentional effort. It takes work and it takes time. Like the song that says, "Take Time To Be Holy," it doesn't happen overnight; it takes time.

If we do all these things, we will reap and enjoy a rewarding and bountiful harvest. We are "the gardener" of our own heart. We are the ones who must tend to our spiritual garden. When the end of our literal garden has come, we rejoice in all the fruit that has been brought in. We enjoy the blessing and reward of all the labor and hard work that went into it. We can now eat and savor those delicious foods for days and weeks to come.

Likewise, if we do the work in the garden of our heart, when we reach Heaven, we will eternally enjoy the benefits of the seeds that were sown, the fruit that grew, and the harvest that was gained.

Oh, how much we can glean from the garden! How many truths and lessons we can be taught about God, this life, and our own heart, right from our own backyard garden. The next time you go out to plant your garden, perhaps you will think of it a little bit differently, not only in physical terms but also in a spiritual aspect as well. There is so much to learn! Whether it's the garden in your yard or the spiritual garden of your heart, I wish you a blessed and successful harvest!

Works Cited

Barnes, a. (n.d.). Galatians 6 Barnes' Notes. https://biblehub.com/commentaries/barnes/galatians/6.htm

Barnes, A. (n.d.-a). *Ephesians 6 - barnes' notes on the whole Bible - bible commentaries.* StudyLight.org. https://www.studylight.org/commentaries/eng/bnb/ephesians-6.html#verse-17

Barnes, A. (n.d.-b). James 5 Barnes' notes. https://biblehub.com/commentaries/barnes/james/5.htm

Easton, M. G. (n.d.). *Fallow-ground - easton's Bible dictionary online.* Bible Study Tools. https://www.biblestudytools.com/dictionaries/eastons-bible-dictionary/fallow-ground.html

Frysh, P. (2024, March 10). *How little doses of sunlight help the body*. WebMD. https://www.webmd.com/a-to-z-guides/ss/slideshow-sunlight-health-effects

Gill, J. (n.d.). Psalm 84 Gill's exposition. https://biblehub.com/commentaries/gill/psalms/84.htm

Greene, O. B. (1966). *The Gospel According To John* (Vol. 2). The Gospel Hour, Inc. (p 253-254)

Ironside, H. A. (2006). *1 & 2 Corinthians: An Ironside Expository Commentary,*. Kregel Publications. (p 72)

Merriam-Webster. (n.d.). *Germinate definition & meaning*. Merriam-Webster. https://www.merriam-webster.com/dictionary/germinate?src=search-dict-box

Spurgeon, C. H. (1869, April 25). *Tearful sowing and joyful reaping*. The Spurgeon Center. https://www.spurgeon.org/resource-library/sermons/tearful-sowing-and-joyful-reaping/#flipbook/

.

www.ingramcontent.com/pod-product-compliance
Lightning Source LLC
Chambersburg PA
CBHW060356050426
42449CB00009B/1767